ENGLAND RULE

Hi, pleased to meet you.

We hope you enjoy our book about the England team!

I'm **VARbot** with all the facts and stats!

SIMON

DAN

WELBECK
CHILDREN'S BOOKS

First published in 2023 by Welbeck Children's Limited.
Reprinted in 2025 by Welbeck Children's Books
An imprint of Hachette Children's Group
Part of Hodder & Stoughton Limited
Carmelite House, 50 Victoria Embankment
London EC4Y 0DZ

An Hachette UK Company
www.hachette.co.uk
www.hachettechildrens.co.uk

Text © 2025 Simon Mugford
Design & Illustration © 2025 Dan Green
ISBN: 978-1-78312-992-8

Writer: Simon Mugford
Designer and Illustrator: Dan Green
Design Manager: Sam James
Senior Commissioning Editor: Suhel Ahmed
Production: Arlene Alexander

Printed in the UK
10 9 8 7 6 5 4 3 2 1

The authorised representative in the EEA is Hachette Ireland,
8 Castlecourt Centre, Dublin 15, D15 XTP3, Ireland (email: info@hbgi.ie)

Statistics and records correct as of March 2023

MIX
Paper | Supporting
responsible forestry
FSC® C104740
FSC
www.fsc.org

FOOTBALL SUPERSTARS

ENGLAND

RULE

SIMON MUGFORD   DAN GREEN

CONTENTS

INTRODUCTION

If you're a fan of the **ENGLAND** men's football team, then this is **DEFINITELY** the book for you!

ENGLAND

Journey through the highs, the lows (and there are plenty of those) the **greatest goals** and **winning moments**.

From **legendary players** and **inspirational managers** to **the massive matches** that your mum and dad, granny or uncle talk about every time **England** play. . .

WELCOME TO . . .

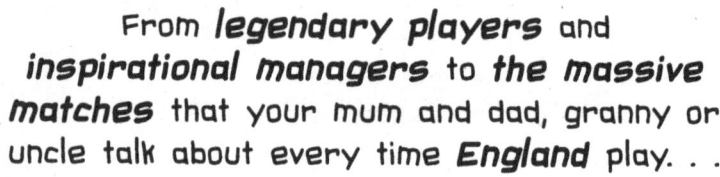

ENGLAND RULE

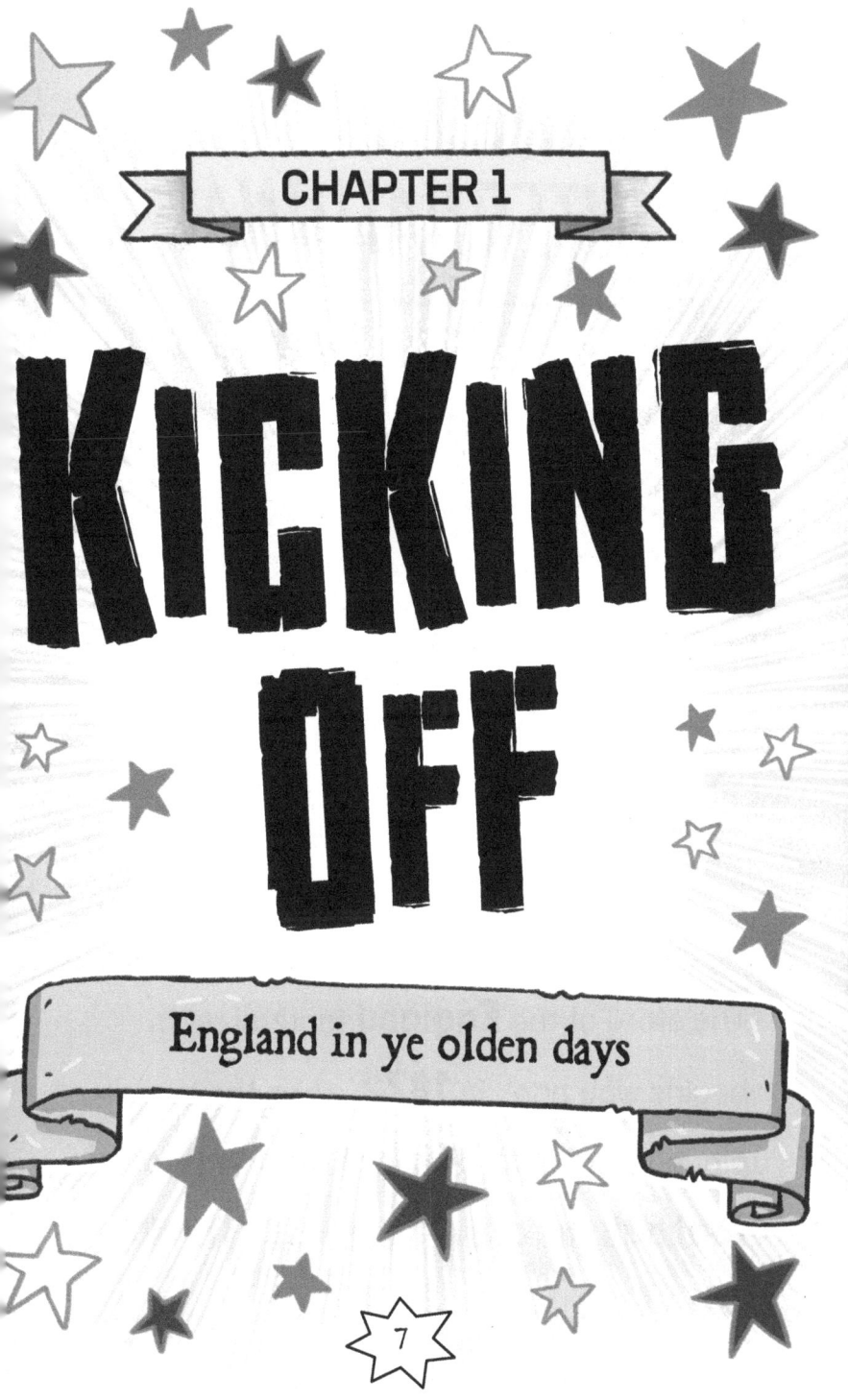

CHAPTER 1

KICKING OFF

England in ye olden days

THE FIRST INTERNATIONAL

The story of the **England** football team begins way back in **1872,** when the team played the **first official international football match** against... **SCOTLAND!**

A crowd of **4,000** watched the match in Glasgow. Scotland began strongly, but England were better in the second half.

By all accounts it was an entertaining game - but it ended in a **0-0 draw.**

The match was organised by **Mr Charles W Alcock,** who selected the England team - and later captained it.

I ALSO STARTED THE **FA CUP!**

And the first **FA Cup final** was also in **1872.**

9

THE WEMBLEY WAY

It's difficult to imagine England without **Wembley!** But before the stadium was built, the team played at different venues around the country.

The stadium opened in **1923.** Before long, its famous **Twin Towers** became a landmark for London and the **'capital of football'.**

This is what Pele called it.

WELCOM TO WIMBERLEE

OI! HUMAN, YOU SPELT IT WRONG

10

England only played **Scotland** at Wembley until 1951, when **Argentina** became the first overseas team to play there.

*England won **2-1**.*

The original Wembley was demolished in **2000,** with the new stadium opening in **2007.**

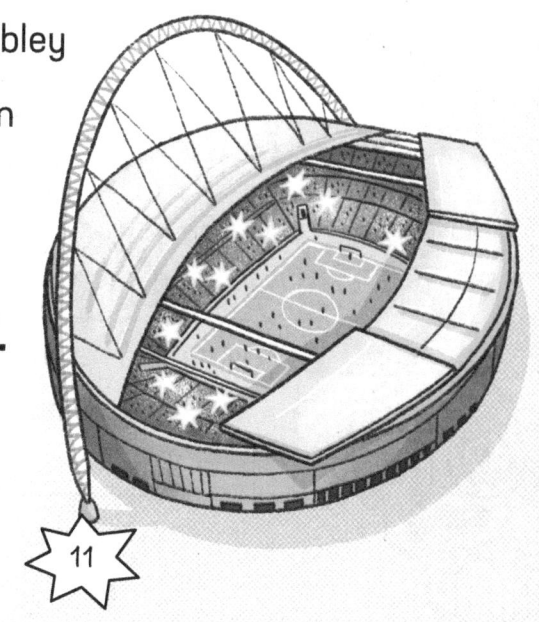

ENGLAND vs THE WORLD

England's second game in the **1950 World Cup** was against the USA. It was billed as **'the Kings of Football'** versus the American 'part-timers'.

It didn't go well. England lost the match **1–0** in one of the biggest World Cup upsets of all time.

England have played the **USA** at the World Cup **twice** since 1950 – in 2010 and 2022 – and drawn both times.

When Hungary played England at Wembley in 1953, they were the number one team in the world – and had the incredible striker **Ferenc Puskas.** The so-called **Match of the Century** ended in a **6–3** loss to England.

Ferenc Puskas
(he scored twice)

YE OLDE LEGENDS

William Kenyon-Slaney was not your average England footballer. He scored England's **first ever** goal - against Scotland in 1873 - and went on to be a colonel in the army and then a politician.

Billy Bassett was a legend at **West Bromwich Albion** - a winger who dribbled and controlled the ball like no one else at the time. He played 16 games for England and scored eight goals.

Steve Bloomer was a **GOAL MACHINE** –

he scored in his first 10 games for England. With 314 First Division goals, he is the second-highest top-flight English scorer in history, behind Jimmy Greaves (357).

He also played baseball for England!

Vivian Woodward

became England's record scorer (29 goals) in 1911 – a record that stood for 47 years. He also captained Great Britain to **Olympic gold** in 1908 and 1912.

Sir Stanley Matthews was speedy, skilful and an awesome crosser of the ball. Super-fit, he played at the highest level until he was **50** and is the oldest England player at 42. The **1953 FA Cup final,** which he almost single-handedly won for Blackpool, is known as the **'Matthews Final.'**

Matthews won the first ever **Ballon d'Or** in **1956.**

He was known as *The Wizard of the Dribble!*

BALLON D'OR 1956

16

CHAPTER 2

THEY THINK IT'S ALL OVER

THE LEGEND OF 1966

THE BOSS

England's terrible performances in the 1950s meant that something needed to change.

Alf Ramsey had played for England, including in the 1953 defeat to Hungary, but had retired to become manager of **Ipswich Town.**

Best team in the world!

IPSWICH TOWN

Ramsey had taken Ipswich from the THIRD DIVISION (now League One) to **ENGLISH CHAMPIONS** in just SIX YEARS - incredible! In 1963, the FA bosses decided Ramsey was the man for England.

"WE WILL WIN THE WORLD CUP."

Ramsey introduced a narrow formation that Ipswich played - the **'Wingless Wonders'.**

It worked . . . wonders?

CHAMPIONS OF THE WORLD

30 JULY 1966

WORLD CUP FINAL, WEMBLEY STADIUM

ENGLAND 4-2 WEST GERMANY *(AET)*

England knocked out **Argentina** and **Portugal** to set up the final with **West Germany**.

England led **2–1,** before a late Germany equaliser took the match to extra-time.

England's third goal was controversial.

The question of whether it **crossed the line**

- or not - has been discussed ever since!

It didn't matter - in the last minute of extra-time,

Geoff Hurst scored again to win it **4–2!**

"SOME PEOPLE ARE ON THE PITCH, *THEY THINK IT'S ALL OVER. IT IS NOW!* IT'S FOUR!"

Kenneth Wolstenholme

96,924 fans watched England's **greatest moment** at Wembley, while 32.3 million people watched it on the telly.

WILL WE EVER SEE IT HAPPEN AGAIN?

HOW TO *LOSE* A WORLD CUP

England may have won the World Cup in 1966, but the trophy was lost - **literally** - earlier that year.

In March 1966, the **Jules Rimet trophy** was on display at an exhibition in London, when it was stolen. The thieves demanded £15,000 from the FA to return it.

22

A week after the theft, **Pickles** was out for a walk with his owner in **South London,** when he found the trophy, wrapped in newspaper.

Pickles was the most **famous dog** in the world - he even got to celebrate the World Cup win with the England team!

LEGENDS OF **66**

Hurst was the **ONLY** player to score a **hat-trick** in a World Cup final until **Kylian Mbappe** did it in **2022**.

ALL GUTS, NO GLORY

THE GLOOM AND DOOM YEARS

IN THE **WILDERNESS**

The **1970s** were not great for England fans. The team travelled to **Mexico** for the 1970 World Cup as champions, but returned early as **West Germany** took their revenge, beating England **3–2** in the quarter-final.

The four games at the 1970 World Cup were their **only** finals matches in the decade.

1972 EUROS

DIDN'T QUALIFY

1974 WORLD CUP

DIDN'T QUALIFY

1976 EUROS

DIDN'T QUALIFY

1978 WORLD CUP

DIDN'T QUALIFY

1980 EUROS

GROUP STAGE EXIT

1982 WORLD CUP

SECOND GROUP STAGE EXIT

THE HAND OF GOD

In 1986, England were back in **Mexico** for another World Cup quarter-final, this time against Argentina. This infamous fixture is remembered for **TWO GOALS** by the one-and-only **Diego Maradona**.

Early in the second half Argentina went ahead, as Maradona appeared to head the ball past keeper Peter Shilton. Except he didn't use his head . . .

Moments later Maradona shimmied past

FOUR England players to score the **GOAL**

OF THE CENTURY.

Gary Lineker scored a late goal for England.

And he won the *Golden Boot!*

ITALIAN RENAISSANCE

The 1990 World Cup in Italy made English fans fall in love with football again. Manager **Bobby Robson** led the team to the semi-final - their first since 1966 - where they played . . . **West Germany.**

When **Paul Gascoigne** received a yellow card, it meant he would **miss the final** if England went through. When he started to cry, 'Gazza' became one of the most famous people on the planet . . .

England went behind, but **Gary Lineker** equalised to force extra-time. Both sides missed chances, and so the match went to a **PENALTY SHOOT-OUT . . .**

WADDLE'S *WOBBLE*

This was the first-ever World Cup penalty shoot-out England had been in. And it didn't end well. **Stuart Pearce's** spot-kick was saved, while **Chris Waddle** sent his over the bar. England were out. And so began **30 YEARS of penalty shoot-out pain** for England . . .

Chris Waddle

26 JUNE 1996

EUROS SEMI-FINAL, WEMBLEY

GERMANY 1-1 ENGLAND

(LOST 6-5 ON PENALTIES)

Gareth Southgate

NO!

30 JUNE 1998

OH NO!

WORLD CUP ROUND OF 16, SAINT-ETIENNE

ARGENTINA 2-2 ENGLAND

(LOST 4-3 ON PENALTIES)

David Batty

OH MAN!

24 JUNE 2004

EUROS QUARTER-FINAL, LISBON

PORTUGAL 2-2 ENGLAND

(LOST 6-5 ON PENALTIES)

Darius Vassell

1 JULY 2006

NOT AGAIN!

WORLD CUP QUARTER-FINAL, GELSENKIRCHEN

ENGLAND 0-0 PORTUGAL

(LOST 3-1 ON PENALTIES)

Steven Gerrard

CHAPTER 4

IT'S COMING HOME

THE STORY OF EURO 96

ENGLAND AT **HOME**

In **1996,** 30 years after that famous World Cup win, England hosted another major tournament, **the European Championship.**

The **Premier League,** which started in **1992** and attracted international stars, had grown into the most exciting league on the planet. The world was watching England - and the fans couldn't wait

ENGLAND

COME ON ENGLAND!

38

HOME NATION

England would play all their matches at **Wembley.**

WOO HOO!

EL TEL

Terry Venables was the England manager. He'd won **La Liga** as the head coach of Barcelona and the **FA Cup** with Tottenham. He was very popular and the players loved him!

THREE LIONS ON A SHIRT

It was at **EURO 96** that we first we heard the words, **"IT'S COMING HOME!"** being sung in stadiums, pubs and living rooms across the country.

THREE LIONS, by comedians David Baddiel and Frank Skinner, and the rock band The Lightning Seeds was the official England song for the tournament.

It is still THE England anthem to sing . . .

SONG SUBS

WORLD CUP WILLIE

Lonnie Donegan, 1966

WORLD IN MOTION

New Order, 1990

VINDALOO

Fat Les, 1998

WE'RE ON THE BALL

Ant & Dec, 2002

WEMBLEY WINNERS

The big match in the group was against old rivals Scotland. **Alan Shearer** scored, **David Seaman** saved a penalty, and **Paul Gascoigne** scored one of the greatest England goals ever. **2–0!**

Alan Shearer

see page 86

Against the Netherlands, England were at their best. **Alan Shearer** and **Teddy Sheringham** bagged two goals each - **4–1!**

Teddy Sheringham

Spain were the quarter-final opponents.

It ended in a penalty shoot-out . . . **OH NO!**

But Seaman was the hero again as

England **WON!**

And then they faced . . . **Germany**

(yep, again) in the semi-final.

Gulp!

AND LOSERS . . .

Thanks to Shearer, England led after just **THREE** minutes, but it ended at **1–1** again.

With the shoot-out score **6–5** to Germany, England needed a volunteer to take the **sixth penalty** . . . and **Gareth Southgate** put his hand up.

He took his **shot** . . .

BINK!

But his penalty was **saved** . . .

"I'LL REMEMBER THIS..."

44

CHAPTER 5

THE BIG MATCH

THE GREATEST ENGLAND GAMES

16 JUNE 1982

WORLD CUP ROUND GROUP STAGE, BILBAO

ENGLAND 3-1 FRANCE

England roared into the **1982 World Cup**, taking the lead in their opening game against **Michel Platini's** France inside one minute, thanks to a **Bryan Robson** goal.

France pulled one back, but another goal from Robson and a third from **Paul Mariner** gave the **Three Lions** a famous win.

Ipswich legend Paul Mariner

England won **ALL THREE** first group matches. In the 1982 World Cup, there was a **SECOND,** three-team group stage, where England drew both matches and ended up going home unbeaten.

GUTTED!

Passions ran high in this game, the first World Cup meeting between the two sides since the **Hand of God** incident in 1986.

Ten minutes in and it was 1-1, thanks to penalties from **Gabriel Batistuta** and **Alan Shearer**.

Minutes later, 18-year-old **Michael Owen** scored an incredible solo goal to give England the lead. **2-1!**

See page 88

BOOM!

Javier Zanetti made it 2-2 just before the break. **NO WAY!**

The second half is remembered for the red card **David Beckham** got for for kicking Diego Simeone. England were down to 10 men but held on. Sol Campbell's late header was ruled out and this blistering night of high drama ended in **penalty shoot-out pain.**

1 SEPTEMBER 2001

WORLD CUP QUALIFIER, MUNICH

GERMANY 1-5 ENGLAND

England were still hurting from those penalty shoot-out defeats against Germany in **1990** and **1996.** They had also lost the first World Cup qualifier against Germany (the final match at the old Wembley Stadium) a year before this game.

So this match was a BIG one . . .

Germany went ahead after just **SIX** minutes.

Here we go again.

But then, **Michael Owen** bagged a **hat-trick** while **Steven Gerrard** and **Emile Heskey** made it **5–1**.

INCREDIBLE!

Germany had been beaten at home in one of the **greatest nights** for English football.

The first half was goalless, but **Harry Kane** put England ahead shortly after the break.

KA-POW!

English hearts sank as Colombia's injury-time equaliser forced an **extra 30 minutes** and the all-too familiar penalty shoot-out.

But it was different this time. Even when **Jordan Henderson** missed his spot-kick, England kept it together.

Colombia missed one, **Jordan Pickford** saved one and England **WON** a World Cup penalty shoot-out **for the first time.**

GLORIOUS STUFF!

29 JUNE 2021

EURO 2020 ROUND OF 16, WEMBLEY

ENGLAND 2-0 GERMANY

It had been **55 years** since England had beaten Germany in a **knockout match** at a major competition. And with fans back watching tournament football for the first time since Covid, it was an emotional fixture.

EN-GER-LAND!

It was tense, tight, end-to-end stuff. When **Raheem Sterling** finally got the breakthrough goal, the crowd - and the country - erupted into **wild celebrations.**

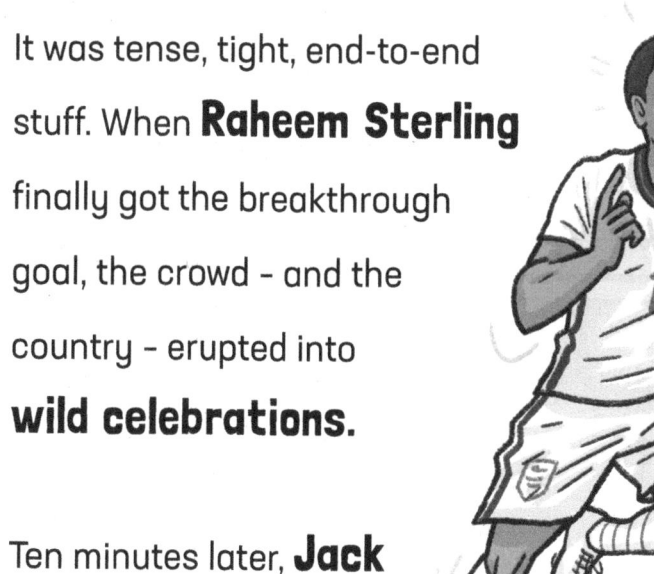

Ten minutes later, **Jack Grealish** set **Harry Kane** up beautifully to head home - **2–0!**

David Beckham and Ed Sheeran were in the crowd

ENGLAND'S *BIG* WINS

Some of the **biggest goal margins** in England history . . .

YEAR	OPPONENT	SCORE
1882	IRELAND	13-0
1907	NETHERLANDS	12-2
1908	AUSTRIA	11-1
1947	PORTUGAL	10-0
1964	USA	10-0
1982	LUXEMBOURG	9-0
2018	PANAMA	6-1
2021	SAN MARINO	10-0
2022	IRAN	6-2

CHAPTER 6

MEET THE BOSS

THE MANAGERS WITH THE MOST (AND LEAST)

WALTER WINTERBOTTOM

YEARS MANAGED: *1946-1962*

BEST RESULT: *1954 AND 1962 WORLD CUP QUARTER-FINALS*

58

England didn't have a manager before **Walter Winterbottom** was appointed. As manager he coached the players but he didn't pick the team. That was done by an FA committee.

Not only was he the **FIRST** England manager, Winterbottom is also the **YOUNGEST** (33 when he took the job) and the **LONGEST SERVING** (16 years).

England qualified for **four World Cups** under Winterbottom, but with little success. He did manage to convince the FA that the next manager - **Alf Ramsey** - should pick the team.

AND THAT WORKED OUT OKAY!

59

RON GREENWOOD

YEARS MANAGED: *1977-1982*

BEST RESULT: *1982 WORLD CUP SECOND GROUP STAGE*

Qualifying for the 1982 World Cup (England's first for 12 years) was a great achievement for Greenwood. Exiting it **unbeaten** having played **France, West Germany** and **Spain** surely makes him England's unluckiest boss!

Greenwood is remembered for selecting England's first black player, **Viv Anderson,** in 1978. A big deal at the time.

He also gave debuts to two other black players - **Laurie Cunningham** and **Cyril Regis**.

Laurie Cunningham

Cyril Regis

BOBBY ROBSON

YEARS MANAGED: *1982-1990*

BEST RESULT: *1990 WORLD CUP SEMI-FINAL*

Bobby Robson's path to the England job was the same as **Alf Ramsey's.** As the manager of **Ipswich Town,** he won the **FA Cup** in 1978 and the **UEFA Cup** in 1981.

Tractor Boys rule!

IPSWICH F.C.

62

Robson was the manager when Maradona scored his **'Hand of God'** goal.

"IT WASN'T THE HAND OF **GOD**, IT WAS THE HAND OF **A RASCAL**."

And in **1990** he led England to their first World Cup semi-final since 1966, where he looked after a tearful **Gazza** and a gutted **Chris Waddle.**

SNIFF!

A legend and a gentleman of the game.

GRAHAM TAYLOR

YEARS MANAGED: *1990-1994*

BEST RESULT: *EURO 1992 GROUP STAGE*

Taylor lived and breathed football, but failing to qualify for the **1994 World Cup** *ended his time as manager.*

TERRY VENABLES

YEARS MANAGED: *1994-1996*

BEST RESULT: *EURO 1996 SEMI-FINAL*

'El Tel' was funny and very popular with the public – and knew how to get the best out of the team.

GLENN HODDLE

YEARS MANAGED: *1996-1999*

BEST RESULT: *1998 WORLD CUP ROUND OF 16*

Hoddle was a **smart manager** and good at tactics, but failed to get the best out of a star-studded squad.

KEVIN KEEGAN

YEARS MANAGED: *1999-2000*

BEST RESULT: *EURO 2000 GROUP STAGE*

Keegan had a poor record, but his team did beat **Germany** at **EURO 2000!**

SVEN GORAN-ERIKSSON

YEARS MANAGED: *2001-2006*

BEST RESULTS: *2002 WORLD CUP, EURO 2004, 2006 WORLD CUP QUARTER-FINALS*

England's **first** non-English manager. Sven got the best results in more than a decade, but with players like **Wayne Rooney** and **David Beckham,** he was expected to win trophies.

STEVE McCLAREN

YEARS MANAGED: *2006-2007*

BEST RESULT: *A 1-1 DRAW AGAINST BRAZIL IN A FRIENDLY.*

*Remembered for failing to qualify for **EURO 2008** while standing under an umbrella in the rain at Wembley.*

FABIO CAPELLO

YEARS MANAGED: *2007-2012*

BEST RESULT: *2010 WORLD CUP ROUND OF 16*

*The former **Real Madrid** coach did well in qualifiers but England were **REALLY** poor at the **2010 World Cup** and were knocked out by Germany!*

ROY HODGSON

YEARS MANAGED: *2012-16*

BEST RESULT: *EURO 2012 QUARTER-FINAL*

A gentleman and great footballing man, but losing to Iceland at **EURO 2016** meant he had to go.

SAM ALLARDYCE

YEAR MANAGED: *2016*

BEST RESULT: *WORLD CUP QUALIFIER WIN*

Allardyce was manager for just **67 days** before he had to leave for breaking FA rules. **Doh!**

CHAPTER 7

LIONS LEGENDS

GREAT PLAYERS WHO WORE THE BADGE

JIMMY GREAVES

POSITION: *STRIKER*

YEARS: *1959-67*

Greaves is the scorer of **357** top-flight goals in English football – a record. Tragically, he missed out on the 1966 World Cup final after getting injured in the group stage.

WHOMP!

Greaves was **finally** given a winners' medal in 2009.

PETER SHILTON

POSITION: *GOALKEEPER*

YEARS: *1970-1990*

Shilton is England's most capped player with **125 appearances**. *The two-times European Cup winner with Nottingham Forest was between the sticks when England played Maradona's Argentina at the 1986 World Cup.*

TERRY BUTCHER

POSITION: *CENTRE-BACK*

YEARS: *1980-90*

The **Ipswich Town legend** *memorably played with a blood-soaked, bandaged head in a World Cup qualifier in 1989 before captaining England at the tournament in 1990.*

BRYAN ROBSON

POSITION: *MIDFIELDER*

YEARS: *1980-91*

'Captain Marvel'
captained England
65 times and scored
26 goals, including one after just **27 seconds**
against France in the 1982 World Cup.

JOHN BARNES

POSITION: *WINGER*

YEARS: *1983-95*

*The superbly talented
winger, who enjoyed
massive success at **Liverpool,** famously
scored a beautiful goal against Brazil in a
1984 friendly at the Maracana stadium.*

GARY LINEKER

POSITION: *STRIKER*

YEARS: *1984-1992*

*The **player-turned-sports presenter** played at the 1986 and 1990 World Cups, scoring a total of **NINE** goals – more than any other player to wear an England shirt.*

BOFF!

PAUL GASCOIGNE

POSITION: *ATTACKING MIDFIELDER*

YEARS: *1988-98*

'**Gazza**' was the most gifted England player of his time, known for his moments of magic, but also troubled times off the pitch. It's difficult to imagine England 's memorable matches at the **1990 World Cup** and **EURO 96** without him.

CRACK!

TONY ADAMS

POSITION: *CENTRE-BACK*

YEARS: *1988-2002*

The inspirational Arsenal man captained England and is the only England player to play at international tournaments in three different decades.

He also appeared on *Strictly Come Dancing!*

ALAN SHEARER

POSITION: *STRIKER*

YEARS: *1992-2000*

Still the Premier League's **record scorer,** *Shearer was fantastic for England at EURO 96, where his* **FIVE** *tournament goals won him the* **Golden Boot.**

PAUL INCE

POSITION: *MIDFIELDER*

YEARS: *1992-2000*

'**The Guvnor**' became the first black player to captain England in 1993. He's also remembered (like Terry Butcher) for playing a match with his head in bandages!

RIO FERDINAND

POSITION: *CENTRE-BACK*

YEARS: *1997-2011*

The one-time world's **most expensive** defender played 81 times for England and appeared at three World Cups.

TEDDY SHERINGHAM

POSITION: *STRIKER*

YEARS: *1993-2002*

With Alan Shearer, Sheringham formed a formidable strike duo known as **SAS,** famously scoring two goals each against the Netherlands at EURO 96.

DAVID BECKHAM

POSITION: *MIDFIELDER*

YEARS: *1998-2008*

A global icon known for his incredible **bending crosses** and **free-kicks,** Beckham appeared at three World Cups and two EUROs, earning 115 caps and scoring 17 goals.

FWOMF!

MICHAEL OWEN

POSITION: *STRIKER*

YEARS: *1998-2008*

Owen burst on to the international scene as an **18-year-old** and became the only England player to score at four separate international tournaments.

STEVEN GERRARD

POSITION: *MIDFIELDER*

YEARS: *2000-2014*

Gerrard's first England goal came in the unforgettable **5-1** win over Germany in 2001 and he went on to play at three EUROs and three World Cups.

WAYNE ROONEY

POSITION: *FORWARD/MIDFIELDER*

YEARS: *2003-2018*

*Rooney was an England fixture for about 15 years. The country's **youngest goalscorer** at 17, he is second in England's list of all-time top scorers with 53 goals.*

CHAPTER 8

HOT SHOTS

THE GREATEST ENGLAND GOALS

PLATTY *POWER*

26 JUNE 1990

ENGLAND 1-0 BELGIUM

In the last minutes of extra-time in this World Cup round of 16 match, **Paul Gascoigne** made a fantastic run.

He was fouled and took the resulting free kick, looping the ball over to the edge of the box, where **David Platt** ... swivelled like an acrobat and volleyed the ball into the net. **BOOM!** An absolute beauty.

Cue wild celebrations and **silly dances.** Even **Bobby Robson** was having a jig on the touchline.

YIPPEE!

GAZZA'S GENIUS

Deep into the second half, **David Seaman** had just denied Scotland a chance to equalise by saving a penalty. The keeper quickly sent the ball to the other end of the pitch . . .

FUMPF!

It was soon with **Paul Gascoigne**, who in a moment of pure magic, lobbed the ball OVER Colin Hendrie, and then volleyed it past Andy Goram to score. **Simply incredible.**

Gascoigne

THE **BEST** GOAL IN ENGLAND'S HISTORY.

And the celebration was memorable, too!

SPLOOSH!

DUTCH MASTERED

18 JUNE 1996

NETHERLANDS 1-4 ENGLAND

Shearer had already opened the scoring with a penalty and Teddy Sheringham had added another. **England were flying.**

As Paul Gascoigne skilfully drew defenders towards him in the box, he gave it to Sheringham who dinked it to Shearer and **OOF – IT'S A NETBUSTER!**

THWACK!

A **BRILLIANT** TEAM GOAL FROM ONE OF ENGLAND'S **FINEST PERFORMANCES.**

BOY WONDER GOAL

This World Cup classic began in frenzy, with a **penalty** converted by each team inside the first **10 minutes**.

The England fans were still celebrating Alan Shearer's equaliser, when David Beckham sent **18-year-old Michael Owen** off on an awesome solo run.

BOMP!

88

At **incredible speed,** Owen sprinted
and shimmied past two defenders before
hammering the ball into the net.

JUST MAGNIFICENT.

89

BECKHAM BENDS IT

England needed to draw this home match to qualify for the **2002 World Cup** . . . But they were **2–1** behind at 90 minutes . . .

Then England won a free-kick way outside the box. There was only one man for this one – **David Beckham.**

He stepped up and **- POW -** the ball rocketed (and bent) over the heads of everyone, including the keeper and into the net.

Beckham

POW!

YAY, GO GOLDEN BALLS!

Victoria Beckham celebrating

RASHFORD RULES

29 NOVEMBER 2022

WALES 0-3 ENGLAND

The build-up to this game was **MASSIVE** – two home nations facing each other at the World Cup. And in the first half, England were **drawing 0–0.**

Oh-no.

Whatever **Gareth Southgate** said to **Marcus Rashford** at half-time did the trick. England won a free-kick outside the area shortly after the break.

92

SLAM!

Rashford stepped up - and **hammered it** home, kick-starting England into life.

Phil Foden scored a minute later and Rashford added another.

SENSATIONAL!

93

BEST OF THE REST

– FIVE MORE TOP GOAL GETTERS

PLAYER	YEAR	OPPONENT	GOAL
JOE COLE	2006	SWEDEN *World Cup*	THUMPING VOLLEY
BOBBY CHARLTON	1966	MEXICO *World Cup*	LONG-RANGE SCREAMER
JACK WILSHERE	2015	SLOVENIA *EUROS qualifier*	LEFT FOOT CRACKER
JOHN BARNES	1984	BRAZIL *Friendly*	BRILLIANT MAZY RUN
GRAEME LE SAUX	1995	BRAZIL *Friendly*	SWEET LONG-RANGE VOLLEY

CHAPTER 9

YOU'RE THE ONE

THE GARETH SOUTHGATE ERA

A NEW START

In 2016, **Gareth Southgate** became England's 20th manager. The team had only recently been dumped out of **EURO 2016** by **Iceland.** There was a lot of work to do.

Southgate's England topped their group to qualify for the **2018 World Cup.** But even then, hopes were not high . . .

RUSSIA WITH LOVE

But in Russia, England surprised everyone, hammering **Panama 6–1,** and beating **Colombia** in a penalty shoot-out.

Then England got past **Sweden** (having never beaten them at a World Cup before) to reach their **first** World Cup semi-final since 1990.

Croatia got the better of England and they missed out on a place in the final - **again.**

The country was disappointed, but they were **proud.** Southgate had made the team entertaining - **and likeable!**

It felt good to be an England fan again!

WHOOP!

99

FINALLY...A FINAL

By the time **EURO 2020** came around,

the excitement was unbearable.

> It was delayed because of the *Covid pandemic.*

England beat **Croatia** (revenge for 2018), then knocked out **Germany** (yes, really), **Ukraine** and **Denmark** to reach a first **FINAL** since 1966.

WOW!

The dramatic final against **Italy** at **Wembley** ended in **ANOTHER** penalty shoot-out defeat, but Southgate rallied the players.

WORLD CUP 2022

Highlights of England's campaign in Qatar.

21 NOVEMBER 2022

WORLD CUP GROUP B

ENGLAND 6-2 IRAN

*The Three Lions couldn't have started better as they totally outclassed Iran. **Jude Bellingham** scored his first goal for England, **Bukayo Saka** scored two, while **Raheem Sterling, Marcus Rashford** and **Jack Grealish** all got on the score sheet. Job done.*

4 DECEMBER 2022

WORLD CUP ROUND OF 16

ENGLAND 3-0 SENEGAL

*Senegal were without star Sadio Mane and England took full advantage. Bellingham controlled the game, setting up **Jordan Henderson** to score, while **Harry Kane** and **Saka** added two more.*

10 DECEMBER 2022

WORLD CUP QUARTER-FINAL

ENGLAND 1-2 FRANCE

*Coming up against the reigning champions was never going to be easy. But **England were brilliant.** Some poor refereeing, bad luck and Kane's missed penalty saw them go home.*

Surely a trophy can't be far away?

103

HARRY KANE

DATE OF BIRTH: **28 JULY 1993**

POSITION: **CENTRE-FORWARD**

CLUB: **TOTTENHAM HOTSPUR**

CAPS: **82**

GOALS: **55**

VALUE: **£80 MILLION**

ON THE PITCH:

"SIMPLY ONE OF THE BEST STRIKERS IN THE WORLD"

RAHEEM **STERLING**

DATE OF BIRTH: **8 DECEMBER 1994**

POSITION: **WINGER / FORWARD**

CLUB: **CHELSEA**

CAPS: **82**

GOALS: **20**

VALUE: **£62 MILLION**

ON THE PITCH:

"A SPEEDY DRIBBLER WHO CREATES AND SCORES GOALS"

BUKAYO **SAKA**

DATE OF BIRTH: **5 SEPTEMBER 2001**

POSITION: **WINGER/MIDFIELDER**

CLUB: **ARSENAL**

CAPS: **26**

GOALS: **8**

VALUE: **£90 MILLION**

ON THE PITCH:

"INSPIRATIONAL. MATURE. ONE OF THE FINEST YOUNG PLAYERS RIGHT NOW"

JUDE *BELLINGHAM*

DATE OF BIRTH: 29 JUNE 2003

POSITION: MIDFIELDER

CLUB: BORUSSIA DORTMUND

CAPS: 24

GOALS: 1

VALUE: £100 MILLION

ON THE PITCH:

"PIVOTAL TO THE TEAM AND A FUTURE ENGLAND CAPTAIN"

JACK GREALISH

DATE OF BIRTH: **10 SEPTEMBER 1995**

POSITION: **WINGER/ATTACKING MIDFIELDER**

CLUB: **MANCHESTER CITY**

CAPS: **31**

GOALS: **2**

VALUE: **£62 MILLION**

ON THE PITCH:

"STYLISH PLAYMAKER WITH SLICK SKILLS. FAN FAVOURITE"

MARCUS *RASHFORD*

DATE OF BIRTH: **31 OCTOBER 1997**

POSITION: **FORWARD**

CLUB: **MANCHESTER UNITED**

CAPS: **51**

GOALS: **15**

VALUE: **£50 MILLION**

ON THE PITCH:

"A COMPOSED, BRILLIANT ATTACKING PLAYER - AND AN INSPIRATION"

MASON *MOUNT*

DATE OF BIRTH: **10 JANUARY 1999**

POSITION: **ATTACKING/CENTRAL MIDFIELDER**

CLUB: **CHELSEA**

CAPS: **36**

GOALS: **5**

VALUE: **£66 MILLION**

ON THE PITCH:

"VERSATILE ACROSS MIDFIELD, BRILLIANT AT GETTING INTO SPACE"

PHIL FODEN

DATE OF BIRTH: **28 MAY 2000**

POSITION: **MIDFIELDER**

CLUB: **MANCHESTER CITY**

CAPS: **23**

GOALS: **3**

VALUE: **£100 MILLION**

ON THE PITCH:

"AN INCREDIBLE YOUNG TALENT. THE FUTURE OF ENGLAND"

JORDAN **PICKFORD**

DATE OF BIRTH: **7 MARCH 1994**

POSITION: **GOALKEEPER**

CLUB: **EVERTON**

CAPS: **52**

GOALS: **0**

VALUE: **£25 MILLION**

ON THE PITCH:

"A TERRIFIC, AGILE, NATURAL SHOT-STOPPER. A WORLD-CLASS KEEPER"

CHAPTER 10

THE BACK PAGES

THE PICK OF THE STATS

ENGLAND'S TEN TOP SCORERS

PUTTING THE BALL IN THE BACK OF THE NET

1ST  **HARRY KANE**
CAPS *82*

GOALS **55**

NEWSFLASH: Kane became England's all-time top scorer (with his 54th goal) on 23 March 2023 in a **EURO 2024** qualifier against Italy.

2ND  **WAYNE ROONEY**
CAPS *120*

GOALS **53**

3RD  **BOBBY CHARLTON**
CAPS *106*

GOALS **49**

4TH  **GARY LINEKER**
CAPS *80*

GOALS **48**

5TH  **JIMMY GREAVES**
CAPS *57*

GOALS
44

6TH  **MICHAEL OWEN**
CAPS *89*

GOALS
40

JOINT
7TH  **TOM FINNEY**
CAPS *76*

GOALS
30

 **NAT LOFTHOUSE**
CAPS *33*

 **ALAN SHEARER**
CAPS *63*

8TH  **FRANK LAMPARD**
CAPS *106*

GOALS
29

MOST CAPPED PLAYERS

RANK	PLAYER	CAPS	YEARS
1	Peter Shilton	125	1970–1990
2	Wayne Rooney	120	2003–2018
3	David Beckham	115	1996–2009
4	Steven Gerrard	114	2000–2014
5	Bobby Moore	108	1962–1973
6	Ashley Cole	107	2001–2014
7=	Bobby Charlton	106	1958–1970
	Frank Lampard	106	1999–2014
9	Billy Wright	105	1946–1959
10	Bryan Robson	90	1980–1991

MOST CLEAN SHEETS

- THE TEN BEST SHOT-STOPPERS

RANK	PLAYER	CS	CAPS	%
1	Peter Shilton	66	125	0.53
2	Joe Hart	43	75	0.57
3	David Seaman	40	75	0.53
4	Gordon Banks	35	73	0.48
5	Ray Clemence	27	61	0.44
6	Chris Woods	26	43	0.60
7=	Paul Robinson	24	41	0.59
	Jordan Pickford	24	50	0.48
9	David James	21	53	0.40
10	Nigel Martyn	13	23	0.57

MOST **HAT-TRICKS**

– SCORING THREE GOALS OR MORE IN A MATCH

RANK	PLAYER	HAT-TRICKS
1	Jimmy Greaves	6
2=	Gary Lineker	5
	Harry Kane	5
3=	Vivian Woodward	4
	Bobby Charlton	4
4	Stan Mortensen	3
5=	Fred Spiksley	2
	Steve Bloomer	2
	Dixie Dean	2
	George Camsell	2
	Tommy Lawton	2
	Tommy Taylor	2
	Geoff Hurst	2
	Michael Owen	2

TEN TOP CLUBS
FOR ENGLAND PLAYERS

- BIGGEST PLAYER PROVIDERS

RANK	TEAM	PLAYERS
1	TOTTENHAM HOTSPUR	78
2=	ASTON VILLA	76
	CORINTHIAN	76
4	LIVERPOOL	74
5=	MANCHESTER UNITED	70
	EVERTON	70
7	ARSENAL	68
8	CHELSEA	54
9	MANCHESTER CITY	52
10	BLACKBURN ROVERS	48

THE **BEST** OF THE REST ...

TALLEST PLAYER
PETER CROUCH 2.1M *(also Fraser Forster)*

SHORTEST PLAYER
FANNY WALDEN 1.57M

HIGHEST SCORING SUB
JERMAINE DEFOE *(7 GOALS)*

MOST RED CARDS
WAYNE ROONEY

DAVID BECKHAM *(BOTH 2)*

MOST YELLOW CARDS

DAVID BECKHAM *19*

YOUNGEST PLAYER

THEO WALCOTT *17 YEARS, 75 DAYS*

OLDEST PLAYER

STANLEY MATTHEWS
42 YEARS, 103 DAYS

MOST PENALTY SHOOT-OUT SAVES

JORDAN PICKFORD *3 SAVES*

QUIZ TIME!

How much do you know about the **ENGLAND FOOTBALL TEAM?** Try this quiz to find out, then test your friends!

1. Which team did England play in the first international match?

----

2. In which World Cup did England lose 1-0 to the USA?

----

3. Who was the England manager at the 1966 World Cup?

----

4. Which player scored a hat-trick at the 1966 World Cup final?

----

5. Which player scored a sensational solo goal against Argentina in 1998?

----

6. And which player was sent off in the same match?

----

7. For which tournament was the song Three Lions written for?

----

8. Which player has scored the most World Cup goals?

----

9. In which competition did England play their first major final since 1966?

----

10. How many goals did England score against Iran at the 2022 World Cup?

The answers are on the next page *but no peeking!*

ANSWERS

1. Scotland
2. 1950
3. Alf Ramsey
4. Geoff Hurst
5. Michael Owen

6. David Beckham
7. EURO 96
8. Gary Lineker
9. EURO 2020
10. Six

ENGLAND WORDS
YOU NEED TO KNOW

World Cup
The biggest tournament for international teams.

EUROS
The major European tournament for international teams.

Cap
An appearance for international side.

Jules Rimet Trophy
The original World Cup trophy.

Ballon d'Or
The award for the year's best footballer in the world.

HAVE YOU READ ANY OF THESE OTHER BOOKS FROM THE SUPERSTARS SERIES?

FOOTBALL SUPERSTARS

   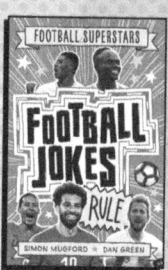 

COLLECT THEM ALL!

SPORTS SUPERSTARS

MORE COMING SOON!

ABOUT THE AUTHORS

Simon's first job was at the Science Museum, making paper aeroplanes and blowing bubbles big enough for your dad to stand in. Since then he's written all sorts of books about the stuff he likes, from dinosaurs and rockets, to llamas, loud music and of course, football. Simon has supported Ipswich Town since they won the FA Cup in 1978 (it's true - look it up) and once sat next to Rio Ferdinand on a train. He lives in Kent with his wife and daughter, a dog and a cat.

Dan has drawn silly pictures since he could hold a crayon. Then he grew up and started making books about stuff like trucks, space, people's jobs, *Doctor Who* and *Star Wars*. Dan remembers Ipswich Town winning the FA Cup but he didn't watch it because he was too busy making a Viking ship out of brown paper. As a result, he knows more about Vikings than football. Dan lives in Suffolk with his wife, son, daughter and a dog that takes him for very long walks.